101 TIPS FOR ASPIRING GRANT WRITERS

Veronica Robbins

CREATIVE
RESOURCES + RESEARCH

203 Elm Street · Woodland, CA 95695

Library of Congress Cataloging-in-Publication Data

101 Tips for Aspiring Grant Writers by Veronica Robbins

ISBN 978-0-9842570-0-3

Printed in the United State of America

For more information about Creative School Resources & Research and the author, Veronica Robbins, please visit us at:

www.grantgoddess.com

ACKNOWLEDGEMENTS

I'd like to thank those whose emotional and moral support made this book (and many of my other endeavors in life) possible. Valiant Robbins, my husband, is primarily responsible for convincing me that I have something to say that could help others succeed as I have succeeded. His constant encouragement and endless reminders kept me on the right track and pushed me to actually finish this project. Kathleen McKeehan, my mother, provided me with many more than 101 tips about life that have put me in a position to write this book and do many other things that I know I would not have done had it not been for her encouragement and example. I owe many thanks to these two very special people.

This book is dedicated to the memory of Kathleen McKeehan,
my first and favorite teacher.

TABLE OF CONTENTS

CHAPTER 3 GOALS AND OBJECTIVES 45

CHAPTER 4 PROGRAM DESIGN 57

CHAPTER 8 BUDGET 103

INTRODUCTION

Written by a professional grant writer, 101 Tips for Aspiring Grant Writers is for those who are just starting out as professional grant writers, individuals who are responsible for grant writing as part of their job, and people with grant writing experience who want some extra help to refine their skills. It is not intended to be the definitive manual on grant writing, but, as the title implies, it is a collection of tips that can be used to help any grant writer improve the quality of his or her applications.

This book is designed to be used as a resource while working through the development of a real grant proposal. It is divided into the sections you will find in a typical Request for Applications (RFA). Convenient "notes" sections on many pages are designed to encourage you to personalize this book by adding your own ideas, thoughts, and experiences to the tips described. 101 Tips for Aspiring Grant Writers is your opportunity to take advantage of a professional's expertise and years of experience and put them to work for you!

CHAPTER 1
GENERAL GRANT WRITING TIPS

TIP 1:
GO INTO THE GRANT WRITING PROCESS WITH CONFIDENCE.

You can do it! Ordinary people win big money grants every day. While there are many professional grant writers out there, just as many (actually, more!) grants are won by folks who do something else for a living and are intent upon earning some additional funds for their respective organizations. If you are diligent about preparing quality applications, you *can* be successful. If you heed the tips in this book, you *will* be successful.

> *"Skill and confidence are an unconquered army..."*
>
> **George Herbert**

TIP 2:
DON'T LET COMPETITION SCARE YOU.

Just because a funding source may be offering only one (or ten or fifty) of a particular type of grant, do not be discouraged from applying. What if *you* would have been the one selected? Also, remember that you learn much from proposals that are not funded. A rejection this year might give you the information needed to be successful next year. If you never try, you'll never succeed.

There are several things to consider before you throw your hat in the ring, so to speak, in a competition offering only a few grants. First, is your plan very closely aligned with the scoring criteria and the overall purpose of the funding opportunity? If so, go for it! If not, consider waiting for another opportunity. A highly competitive application period is not the time to try to fit a square peg into a round hole. Second, are you really prepared to write? Do you have all the materials you need? Are all of the collaborative partners (if partners are required) on board and in agreement about the program? Do you have all of the data you need to build a compelling case for your need for the grant? If not, skip this opportunity and wait for the next one.

Under normal circumstances, none of these conditions would be cause to shy away from a grant competition. In fact, they can test your creativity and flexibility, and success is often possible even when all of the conditions are not perfect. However, in a very competitive situation, you'll need to be sure that you are really ready and in the best position to succeed before you expend huge amounts of energy.

> *"Life shrinks or expands in proportion to one's courage."*
>
> *Anais Nin*

So, just when is a grant competition considered "highly competitive"? That is a very interesting and highly contextual question. In a national competition for a federal grant, one might think that it is a very competitive situation if only forty grants are going to be awarded in a particular competition; however, that is not unusually competitive at all. My "rule" is that if fewer than five grants are going to be awarded in a federal competition, it should be considered "highly competitive." and I won't jump in unless I feel that I have an excellent chance for success. On the other end of the spectrum, if over one hundred grants are being awarded in a federal competition, I consider that situation to be highly favorable for good grant writers.

TIP 3:
READ SOME SUCCESSFUL GRANTS.

Nothing will help you get a handle on what a funding source likes to fund more than reading successful grant proposals. Some funding sources make a few successful proposals available on the Internet as models. You can also ask current grantees if they would mind sharing a copy of their grant proposal with you. They will often be glad to share it with you.

Don't be surprised, though, if successful grantees are not so motivated to share. Their reluctance is not always a result of unwillingness to help you. Many grant applications include information about collaborative partners or the community that could be considered sensitive. The appropriate thing for them to do in that situation would be to redact (black out) all names and sensitive information before providing the document. However, the grantees are just as busy as you are. In fact, they are probably a bit busier because they have been successful in receiving grant funds so now they are busy implementing a new program. Taking time to go through a full proposal and blacking out names just so you can have a sample of a successful grant is probably not at the top of their priority list. Also, if they used a professional grant writer, there may be some questions or confusion regarding whose intellectual property is embodied in the proposal. It is easier for them to say no to you than to resolve that issue.

The truth is that once a grant has been submitted as part of a federal competition, it is probably available to just about anyone who would like to see it through the Freedom of Information Act (FOIA). The FOIA is a law enacted in 1966 that grants public access to government records. Most grant applications submitted to federal agencies can be accessed through the FOIA. Each federal department processes FOIA requests differently, so your best bet is to go to the Website of the agency where you plan to apply, look up the appropriate FOIA policies, and download an application to request information under FOIA. The cost for accessing information this way varies from program to program; however, it is typically either free or very inexpensive (duplication costs only).

Here's the catch—FOIA requests take awhile to process, so if you want to read the applications that were successful last year, you need to make the requests at least eight weeks prior to your grant competition (sooner, if possible). I suggest that if you know you may be interested in applying for a certain type of grant next year, make your FOIA request *now*. If you don't, you'll end up calling previous grantees and begging them for copies of their successful grants. Unfortunately, most will turn you down. A little advance planning can make all the difference.

TIP 4:
VOLUNTEER TO BE A GRANT READER.

Being a grant reader/scorer will help you quickly learn what it takes to get a grant funded. You will learn how scoring systems work, and you will see many examples of grant proposals—some good, some not so good—all of which help you gain some good perspective on writing. You will see many different ways to structure a compelling case, describe research-validated programs and strategies, and write an evaluation plan (something with which most amateur grant writers struggle). State and federal funding sources will often ask for volunteers to read grants, and they usually have an application process. Keep in mind, however, that it is unethical to read or score grants for a competition that you have entered.

The first time I served as a grant reader/scorer was an eye-opening experience. First, I developed a new appreciation for the importance of paying attention to the detail and following the application instructions (more on this below). Next, I was shocked at how "human" the whole process is. For example, those grants that are read first are scrutinized intensively and tend to get lower scores. Those that are read later in the process tend to be "skimmed" and can potentially fare much better than those read earlier in the process. Finally, I was also struck by how much of a role individual bias plays in the grant scoring process. Even though the criteria are very clear (and sometimes even a detailed scoring rubric has been developed), I heard many readers saying things like, "That will never work. We tried that curriculum (or that strategy, or activity), and it didn't work very well." Readers are instructed not to use any criteria other than those officially published as the scoring criteria, but readers are only human. Just like you and me, they carry their experiences and emotional baggage with them.

In spite of this, you will learn so much about grant writing and the scoring process from serving as a reader that you will be glad you did it.

TIP 5:
READ THE INSTRUCTIONS.

While reading the instructions may seem like a simple thing, you would be amazed how many people overlook it. In fact, the number two reason most grant applications are not successful is because the writer did not fully read the instructions (keep reading to learn about the number one reason for grant failure). Read the instructions from start to finish, without stopping. Read the small print and read the parts that look like technical jargon. Read it all. Remember, your success in being funded rests predominantly on how well you respond to what is contained in the Request for Applications (RFA) or Request for Proposals (RFP), so you want to be sure that you thoroughly understand the instructions.

Here's the process I use: First, I skim through the RFP looking for some critical information that will determine if I will be pursing this competition:

- Due date
- Number of grants expected to be awarded
- Minimum and maximum awards (how much money is available?)
- Page limitations of the narrative (this gives me some idea of how much detail will be required in the narrative)
- Required appendices
- Scoring criteria
- Overall purpose of the program

It takes me about ten minutes to go through this initial survey of the application. Then, if I decide to write a proposal in response to this application, I read the entire application from start to finish with my highlighter in hand and some small flag-like sticky notes so I can flag and label important parts of the application for future reference. This second, more detailed reading can take an hour or longer, but it is critical. Grants have been lost because of lack of attention to detail.

TIP 6:
HIGHLIGHT, OR MAKE NOTES OF, THE CRITICAL ELEMENTS OF THE RFA.

Some people incorporate these notes into their outline. Others simply use them as a way to reinforce the important items. Regardless of how you do it, you need to have some way of making notes about what you really need to remember. Highlighting a working copy of the RFA is a common technique used by many professional grant writers. As I mentioned above, I do it. And it makes a big difference.

TIP 7:
READ ADDITIONAL MATERIAL REFERRED TO IN THE RFA.

Sometimes, an RFA will contain a reference to a book, government publication, or Website. These are hints given to you by the funding source, and the difference between being funded or not could depend on reading those hints. There is one state grant that refers readers of an RFA to a Website, and the Website essentially gives away the "secret" to getting funded. Wouldn't you feel awful if you didn't read what was offered?

It is not uncommon for a federal RFA to include pages of Web links to back up information and references. While researching each and every one of those links is tedious, I highly recommend it. At worst, you'll learn something that may help you with your grant or the program you are planning to implement. At best, you may learn something that makes the difference between writing a winning or a losing proposal.

TIP 8:
DO NOT ASSUME THE CURRENT RFA IS THE SAME AS THE LAST.

Many people who have written multiple grants fall into this trap. While it is fairly common for a particular program's RFA to be similar from year to year, this is not always the case. Funding priorities may shift slightly. Sometimes the wording of a criterion is changed just enough to change its focus. In some cases, the page limitation or formatting instructions may change. No matter how well you think you know a funding source or a particular type of grant, Tip #5 (Read the instructions) *always* applies.

I have reviewed grants that did not address the criteria in the current competition at all. When asked about it, the writers admitted that they did not read the scoring criteria in the current RFA; they merely assumed they would be the same as they had been in years past. If the error had not been caught prior to submittal, those proposals would definitely not have been funded.

TIP 9:
ANSWER THE QUESTIONS DIRECTLY.

Sometimes an RFA includes specific questions that you are asked to answer. In other cases, it lists funding criteria and you are asked to write in response to the criteria. Regardless of how it is presented, your task as a grant writer is to respond directly to the questions or the criteria. *The number one error made by aspiring grant writers is insisting on writing what they want to write in spite of what has been asked.* Never forget that the funding source is holding all the cards and your job is to give them the information they need to determine that your organization would be a great place to invest their money. Not responding to the criteria is a sure sign that you are not interested in the funding source's vision, and the funding source will respond to this by refusing to fund your proposal.

One helpful idea is to rephrase the scoring criteria into question form and then simply answer the questions. For example, a scoring criterion may be worded something like this:

The extent to which the applicant demonstrates how the proposed services directly address the needs of children and youth.

Your reworded version might look like this:

How do the proposed services directly address the needs of children and youth?

You may also try to highlight the critical words of each criterion to help you stay focused. It is very easy to get off track. Staying focused will pay off.

TIP 10:
MATCH YOUR IDEA TO A FUNDING SOURCE.

This is a "don't put the cart before the horse" tip. You should have an excellent idea for a program or set of activities that you would like to implement. This is the first step. Then, go looking for a funding source to match that idea. Many people try to do it backwards by finding a funding source and then trying to come up with something to do just to get the money. Or worse—trying to make an idea fit a grant when it is clearly not aligned with the vision of the funding source. You will be *much* more successful if you develop your idea and go searching for funding sources that are appropriate for your idea. There are some professional grant writers who pride themselves on being able to sell any idea to any funding source. Their funding rates are usually fairly low. This does not mean you should not experiment from time to time, but you need to accept that not every funding organization is interested in every idea.

TIP 11:
USE AN OUTLINE.

Everyone's writing style is different. In this age of technology, it is easy to add new ideas to a narrative once it has been drafted. The downside to this is that many people think there is no longer a need to write an outline, but outlines are extremely valuable. They help you to organize your thoughts and the data you are going to present. They help you to clarify the case you are about to make in your mind before you have to deal with putting flowing text to paper. They can also help you see fallacies in logic before you are so far into the concept development phase that going back to reformulate an argument would take an extraordinary amount of time.

Also, keep in mind that most grant applications have a page limit for the proposal narrative. It is difficult enough to completely address the scoring criteria and provide as much detail about your program as

> *"Good order is the foundation of all things."*
>
> *Edmund Burke*

possible while staying within the narrative page limit restrictions. If your text meanders slowly from thought to thought because of poor planning, you'll be in real trouble.

TIP 12:
THE MORE DETAILED YOUR OUTLINE, THE EASIER WRITING THE NARRATIVE WILL BE.

If you take your time and write a very detailed outline, even inserting some good phrases that you'd like to see in the final narrative, your efforts will be rewarded. The bottom line is that you have to conceptualize the proposal at some time. If you don't do it in the outline phase, you'll have to do it later, and it is much easier to add to or take away from an outline.

Don't get stuck by formal outlining techniques that you may have been taught in school. Here's what I do: I create a document that has one page for each of the scoring criteria (narrative sections), and I type the criterion to be addressed (and its point total) at the top of the page. If there are fifteen criteria, my outline document will be fifteen pages long. Then I think about each criterion individually and develop an outline for my response to that criterion on its dedicated page. As much as I love word processing software, I usually make my outline notes by hand. My outline and notes pages typically have arrows, scribbled out text, and abbreviations all over them, but they are clear to me. In fact, by the time I finish outlining, I am usually itching to get started with the writing because the ideas are so clear in my mind that the grant is starting to write itself. If I'm still struggling with how to get started, I may actually draft a paragraph or two, in longhand, on the bottom of the outline page, just to get started.

TIP 13:
WRITE A FIRST DRAFT.

Once the outline is done, sit down and write. Don't worry if you don't have all the information you need; just get started and work your way through the RFA. You can leave blanks and spaces to insert additional information when it is available. Don't worry about spelling or punctuation in this draft—your focus should be on the development of the ideas. You will go back to revise the draft at another time, and you can catch your errors then (see Chapter 9: Editing).

I make it a policy to work through at least two drafts (usually three) before anyone else reviews my work. Draft #1 gets the ideas from the outline on paper. It is full of blanks and notes to myself to look up this or that piece of information. Draft #2 fills in most of those blanks and cleans up most of the typos or incomplete ideas. I usually work through Draft #2 in bits and pieces. Draft #3 is developed from a complete start-to-finish read through, during which I focus on the clarity of the ideas, the degree to which they clearly address the scoring criteria, and the flow of the writing. There may still be some blanks left after Draft #3, but the narrative is now in respectable shape and ready to be shared with others for feedback. It is nowhere near ready to be submitted to a funding source, but I am ready to share it with "critical friends" who can help me improve it and make it the best it can be.

TIP 14:
PLAN THE LENGTH AND DETAIL OF EACH SECTION BY THE POINTS ALLOCATED FOR EACH.

Most state and federal grants tell you exactly how they are going to score each proposal. A certain number of points are allocated to each section (or criterion), and the readers will assign your proposal points based on your responses. Take a close look at how many points will be awarded for each section. If the *design* section is worth fifty points and the *needs* section is worth five points, that is a clear indicator that you should spend much more time and effort providing detail for the design section than for the needs section. It also gives you a general sense for how many pages each section should include. If, in the scenario just described, a total of one hundred points are to be awarded, 50 percent of those will be for the design section; hence, approximately 50 percent of the proposal's pages should be allocated toward the design section. The problem is that it is human nature to want to speak (or write, in this case) more about those things we know well. You probably know a lot about your need and not as much about your proposed solution. Even so, follow the funding source's lead and allocate time and space accordingly. Of course, there will be times when you need to spend more (or fewer) pages on a criterion than the points percentage would suggest. That's okay; just be aware as you are doing it.

NOTES

Chapter 1: General Grant Writing Tips

CHAPTER 2
EXPRESSING YOUR NEED FOR THE GRANT
(Or, Writing The Needs Section)

TIP 15:
USE VERY CLEAR AND CONCISE LANGUAGE.

You are well aware that there are many genres of writing. The type of language that would work very well in a poem probably would not be effective in an automotive repair manual. In grant writing, the rule is to be clear and concise. Because of space limitations, you will be required to put many ideas into a page-limited document. That means if you can say something in twenty words rather than one hundred words, do so. Dig out that old thesaurus and look for words that will allow you to express your complex ideas as directly as possible.

"Do not say a little in many words, but a great deal in a few..."

Pythagoras

TIP 16:
BRUSH UP ON YOUR WRITING SKILLS, IF NECESSARY.

The majority of the tips in this book assume that you possess the basic grammar and punctuation skills necessary to write effectively. If you need to brush up on your basic grammar skills, take the time to do that; it will pay off greatly in the end. No matter how much anyone tells you, "It's the ideas that count, not the writing," you should not turn in a proposal that is filled with spelling, grammatical, or punctuation errors. While you can find errors on occasion in books published by writing experts (because no one is perfect), it is extremely rare to see a successful grant proposal that is filled with errors. The authors of most winning proposals, whether they are professional or amateur writers, have a solid grasp of basic writing skills. If you want to be a successful grant writer, you will first need to be a good writer.

TIP 17:
DO YOUR RESEARCH.

Gather information and data about your organization. Include as much quantitative data as possible. Don't just write, "We have many socioeconomically disadvantaged students in our school," but rather, "Seventy-five percent (75%) of our students are socioeconomically disadvantaged (as measured by free/reduced lunch statistics) and 65% of those students are not fully proficient in English." Gather demographic data for the population you serve as well as achievement data and information about current programs. It is better to have too much data at your fingertips than too little. You can always choose not to use it.

If you find that you do not have much information about your organization, start working now to remedy that situation. For example, many small nonprofit organizations are so busy providing services to their target populations that they often neglect to document those services. If this is the case for your organization, start now to establish procedures and systems to document the services you provide, to whom you provide them, and how effective they have been. That information is extremely valuable.

TIP 18:
COLLECT DATA THAT MATCH THE VISION OF THE FUNDING SOURCE.

If you are applying for a grant to make your school a safer place, the funding source is going to want to see safety-related data. How many crimes were committed on or around the school campus in the last year? By whom? What types of crimes were they? How many discipline referrals were handled at the school (i.e., pre-crime behavior)? Were these disciplinary issues clustered in a certain area (type of offense)? How were they handled? How do you know whether they were handled effectively or not? Are there more incidents during specific times of year (or times of day) than others? Why is this? How many suspensions and expulsions were there in the last year? You would probably want to disaggregate all this information by grade level, gender, and ethnicity. Now, if you were applying for an artist-in-residence grant, you might not need all of this data. You would probably collect different information that would express your need for an arts program.

TIP 19:
GATHER NEEDS EVIDENCE THAT HAS ALREADY BEEN ASSEMBLED.

Other people in your organization have undoubtedly already gathered a significant amount of needs data for other grants or reports. Places to look might include board reports, Websites, and organization action plans. Don't reinvent the wheel. Take advantage of the data others have gathered. The flip side of this tip is to share data you have gathered with others. If you are willing to share what you have collected, others will be willing to share what they have, too.

TIP 20:
BUILD YOUR CASE THOROUGHLY.

Start by presenting some general information about your organization and the clients you serve. Then move on to more specific information. Include comparisons, whenever possible, to county, state, and nationwide populations. Address any specific data required by the funding source. Include data that speak to your need for the specific grant you are writing (see Tip #18). Add the human element to the numbers. Is there any qualitative information you can include? Consider adding a brief anecdotal story or two to illustrate your points. Are there any direct quotes from clients you can include? By the time you are finished with this section, there should be no doubt as to your need for the grant.

Also, don't assume that the readers will understand the implications of the data you have presented. Tell them, in writing, what is important to notice about the data.

TIP 21:

DON'T BE AFRAID TO INCLUDE INFORMATION THAT IS NOT REQUESTED.

If there is a critical issue that affects the effectiveness of your programs, include it in the needs section, even if the funding source has not asked you to do so. Then explain exactly why you are bringing it up.

TIP 22:
INCLUDE GAPS IN SERVICES IN YOUR DISCUSSION OF NEED.

Sometimes what is missing is just as important as what is present. Even if the funding source has not asked you about staff training, the lack of staff training in a particular area may be a significant problem in your organization. In some cases, pointing out that 90 percent of your clients are Spanish-speaking does not tell the whole story until you mention that only 25 percent of your staff speaks Spanish. Now you have demonstrated a need. The simple existence of a condition or a certain population does not, in itself, constitute a need. It is your current inability to serve that population or deal with that condition that constitutes the need.

TIP 23:
THINK TWICE BEFORE INCLUDING A NEED THAT YOU DO NOT PLAN ON ADDRESSING.

The readers will be looking for the match between your identified needs and the strategies you will use to meet those needs. If you spend time in the needs section talking about how lack of transportation is a serious barrier to your clients' ability to access services and then your plan just includes more services but no transportation, you will be in trouble. Even if you do not plan on using funds from that particular grant to address the issue, you need to explain how you will overcome it. Otherwise, leave it out.

Consider developing a notes page where you list all of the needs you identified in the needs section on the left hand side of the page, and all of your proposed solutions on the right. Then draw a line from each need to a solution. If you end with a need that is not linked to a solution (or vice versa), then either your needs have not been clarified well enough or your solutions are not comprehensive enough.

TIP 24:
BE VERY SPECIFIC.

Use numbers whenever possible. Disaggregate the data as much as you can to make your needs very clear. Don't assume the readers know what you mean by terms like "low achieving" and "underperforming." Exactly what do those terms mean in the context of your organization? Also, be sure to fully spell out all acronyms the first time you use them.

If you are participating in a federal competition, be aware that the readers responsible for scoring your proposal will not be from your state. They will not understand your references to your state's programs and regulations unless you explain them. It's a good practice to assume the readers know very little (or nothing) about your program, your community, and your state.

TIP 25:
USE CHARTS AND GRAPHS.

If a picture is worth a thousand words, a graph is worth at least a few hundred. Graphs are easier to read than text. You can communicate more information in three inches of graphics than you can in three inches of text, and space is *always* a consideration when writing a grant. Be careful, though. You'll want to select a chart or graph that does the best job of making your point. And don't forget—be sure to explain, in text, exactly what important information is illustrated by the graph.

Pay attention to appropriate rules for displaying graphs. Always include a title for your graphs and be sure all labels and numbers are clearly visible. If the graph is in color on your computer screen, check to be sure that it is still as clear when it is printed in black and white.

TIP 26:
LABEL ALL CHARTS AND GRAPHS APPROPRIATELY.

Nothing is more annoying to a reader than not being able to figure out a graph. Seeing a bar graph with numbers and multiple colored bars—and no labels—will not do much to help the reader understand your needs. Always default in favor of labeling too much, rather than labeling too little. Don't depend on colors over labels, because the funding source might make black and white copies of your proposals for distribution, making your colors useless. This does not mean that you shouldn't use color if you can, just that you should not rely on it exclusively.

TIP 27:
INCLUDE SURVEY RESULTS.

If your organization has conducted a survey in the last year or so, consider including a summary of those results in the proposal. You may even want to administer a survey to gather information specifically for the proposal on which you are working. When including survey data, be sure to include the number of surveys distributed and the number of surveys returned. If you were able to disaggregate the data, include that information, too. If the RFA allows you to include attachments beyond the narrative page limitations, consider including a brief summary of the survey in the narrative and putting a longer, more detailed, summary in the appendix.

TIP 28:
EXPLAIN THE PROCESS YOU USED TO PRIORITIZE NEEDS.

Did a committee review all of the needs data and determine the priorities and the services to be provided, or did a single person do this? Was a survey administered that asked clients to prioritize their responses? You are asking the readers to follow you from your determination of your needs to your opinion of how to address those needs. You must clearly communicate how you got from point A (the needs) to point B (the services you propose to address the needs).

NOTES

CHAPTER 3
GOALS AND OBJECTIVES

TIP 29:
DEFINE YOUR GOALS AS BROAD STATEMENTS OF PURPOSE.

Objectives are specific, but goals should be broad. Here are some examples of goals:

- To improve the quality of life for our clients.
- To help all students achieve according to high standards.
- To prepare all teachers to meet the needs of their students.
- To promote tolerance.

"You can't go anywhere unless you know where to start and where to go."

Lionel Barrymore

TIP 30:
LINK YOUR PROGRAM GOALS TO OTHER GOALS IN THE ORGANIZATION.

While it is perfectly natural for each of your programs to have program-specific goals, these goals should all be linked to an overall organizational vision. Describe how your program goals are connected to that vision. You may even want to spend some time elaborating on that vision and the role it plays in the current proposal (depending on space constraints).

TIP 31:
SEPARATE GOALS AND OBJECTIVES GRAPHICALLY.

Some people like to list the goals first and then list the objectives separately. Others like to list each goal individually, followed by the objectives that support that goal, before moving on to the next goal. However you like to do it, make sure that it is very clear to the reader which are your goals and which are your objectives. If you don't do this, a reader may confuse the two and deduct some points because "your objectives were not measurable." Of course, all your objectives were measurable, but your goals were not because they were intended to be general, but by the time the reader has deducted points, it is too late for you to explain all that.

There are many ways you can distinguish between the two. You can use graphics (boxes, shading, icons, etc.) or you can use an outline system (goals are assigned whole numbers and objectives are assigned mixed numbers under each objective) like the example below.

1.0	**Goal**			3.0	**Goal**	
	1.1	*Objective*			3.1	*Objective*
	1.2	*Objective*			3.2	*Objective*
2.0	**Goal**			4.0	**Goal**	
	2.1	*Objective*			4.1	*Objective*
	2.2	*Objective*			4.2	*Objective*

TIP 32:
MAKE YOUR OBJECTIVES REALISTIC, BUT SIGNIFICANT.

You will feel pressure when developing your objectives because you want objectives that are challenging enough to make your effort look significant, but that are also achievable. Keep in mind that, in most cases, a funding source will allow you to easily change many of the activities that you originally wrote in the grant proposal once you are implementing the grant, but you will usually be bound to your objectives. Only rarely will you be allowed to alter them. This means that you should give them some serious thought and make sure they are not impossible to achieve. Nothing feels worse than having to report each year that you have failed to meet your objectives—again—especially when you know that you have made excellent progress.

> *The reason most people never reach their goals is that they don't define them, or ever seriously consider them as believable or achievable."*
>
> *Denis Waitley*

TIP 33:
USE MEASURES THAT ARE AVAILABLE TO YOU.

Unless there are specific measures that are required by the funding source, write your objectives with measurement tools that you have available at your site. While you should use existing assessments whenever possible, try adding new assessments that you had been considering implementing anyway. Just be careful not to commit yourself and your organization to the implementation of a new battery of assessments in addition to the implementation of a new program.

Along these same lines, if a funding source requires you to use new assessments, review these assessments (or detailed descriptions of them) prior to submitting your grant proposal. You need to be sure that you are willing to comply with all grant requirements if you accept the funds.

TIP 34:
MAKE SURE EACH OBJECTIVE HAS ALL ITS PARTS.

The most effective outcome objectives are written as standard behavioral objectives. Each objective should have four parts:

- What will be measured?
- When will it be measured?
- How much growth do you expect?
- How you will know that the objective has been achieved?

If any of these parts is missing, consider your objective incomplete.

TIP 35:
DISTINGUISH IMPLEMENTATION OBJECTIVES FROM OUTCOME OBJECTIVES.

Implementation objectives define your targets for implementing the program (e.g., Fifty program participants will be enrolled by June 30, 2010, as measured by intake records) and outcome objectives define your ultimate achievement targets (e.g., Forty students will complete the program each year, as measured by achievement of a passing score on the XYZ exam). Think of it this way: the achievement of an implementation objective proves that you are implementing the program. The achievement of an outcome objective proves that the program works. While implementation objectives are good, outcome objectives guide the true measures of your effectiveness. Generally speaking, funding sources are most interested in your outcome objectives, and when an RFA refers to "Goals and Objectives," it is referring to goals and outcome objectives.

Implementation objectives can also be used, but only when you clearly distinguish them from outcome objectives. Occasionally, a funding source will specifically ask you to list your implementation objectives. In that case, of course, you should follow the directions and provide the requested information, but typically implementation information is provided in the design section of the proposal.

TIP 36:
REVIEW THE FORMAL EVALUATION REQUIREMENTS OF THE FUNDING SOURCE BEFORE FINALIZING YOUR OBJECTIVES.

Since you will be required to demonstrate the degree to which you have achieved your objectives and you will be required to provide specific data to the funding source as part of the national, state, or organizational (if you have a private funding source) evaluation, it makes sense to try to tailor your objectives to the data that will be required for the formal evaluation. Not only does this streamline your planning and help with implementation, it also demonstrates your understanding of the needs and requirements of the funding source. Of course, some of your objectives will reflect purely local needs, but try to combine your objectives with those of the funding source whenever possible.

NOTES

CHAPTER 4
PROGRAM DESIGN

TIP 37:
HAVE A CLEAR VISION OF WHAT YOU WANT TO DO.

One of the biggest mistakes made by aspiring grant writers is not having a clear vision of what they want to do. They may know that they want to implement a literacy program and that it will have something to do with their existing tutorial program, but that's about it. The more clearly you have defined your idea in your mind (and on paper, whenever possible), the easier it will be to put it in a proposal format. Because your space is limited in a proposal, there is little opportunity to explore your ideas. You need to have a clear picture of what you would like to have funded.

My favorite clients are the ones who have a very clear idea of their vision before they pick up the phone to call me. They have thought out exactly what they want to do, how they will do it, why they want to do it that way, whom they will serve, and how they will measure their effectiveness. They have written their ideas on paper, even if it is big chart paper that they used in their planning session.

> *"It must be borne in mind that the tragedy of life does not lie in not reaching your goals, the tragedy lies in not having any goals to reach."*
>
> *Benjamin I. Mays*

I may have to modify their ideas slightly to fit the requirements of a funding source in one or two insignificant areas, but for the most part, they know exactly what they want to do.

My least favorite clients are those who call and say, "Hey, I saw this RFP for money for XYZ programs and we really need WXY (which is related to XYZ, but not exactly the same). Can you help us get that money?"

TIP 38:
FIND A WAY TO SUMMARIZE YOUR DESIGN IN A SINGLE PARAGRAPH OR A LIST OF BULLETED STATEMENTS.

Even if the funding source does not ask for a brief summary at the beginning of the design section, it is usually in your best interests to provide a summary anyway. Remember that it is your primary purpose to help the reader understand exactly what you want to do and a summary is the best way to achieve that. If you are unable to summarize your project in a paragraph, then you have not been clear enough in developing your vision, or perhaps you have a plan that is not focused enough and needs to be trimmed a bit.

TIP 39:
WHENEVER POSSIBLE, INCLUDE A DESIGN GRAPHIC.

You know the saying— "A picture is worth a thousand words." (Didn't I say that already?) Well, a design graphic can go a long way toward helping a reader understand the elements of a comprehensive project. Even a small graphic or a series of icons that connect running themes in the proposal can be very helpful. Unfortunately, sometimes you won't have enough room to include a graphic, but use one whenever you can.

Here are some ideas: Bridge graphics can help you illustrate a link between needs and solutions. Bull's-eye graphics can help you illustrate the concept of targeting a particular need, or the concept of providing multiple layers of service at varying intensity levels. Flow charts can also be very helpful in illustrating how complex processes will work.

> *"Words cannot describe everything. The heart's message cannot be communicated in words...."*
>
> *Ekai*

TIP 40:
BE VERY SPECIFIC IN YOUR DESCRIPTIONS.

Use quantifiable information whenever possible. For example, instead of saying that you are planning to include a parenting education program in your overall project design, say that you plan to serve fifty adults in a parenting education program that is offered weekly on Wednesdays from 5:30 to 8:30 p.m. over a course of fifteen weeks. Include information on the curricula and the instructor(s), if possible, and tell the reader how the parenting education program is connected to the other elements of the project design and how it will help you to achieve your objectives. It is highly unlikely that you will be held responsible for the implementation detail you put in the grant. If you end up offering the course on Thursdays, instead of Wednesdays, it will be fine. If you have any doubt, ask your program officer (or program consultant, whatever the title may be) before you make the change. The point is that you must think it through with sufficient detail before you get the grant to increase the chances that you will get the grant. You can modify the details or negotiate modifications later. Just be sure that you do not put anything in the application narrative that you do not intend to do.

"Words, like glasses, obscure everything which they do not make clear."

Joseph Joubert

TIP 41:

DON'T BE AFRAID TO USE SUBHEADINGS TO BREAK UP THE DESIGN SECTION.

You generally should respond to all of the program criteria in order; however, there is nothing wrong with adding subheadings within those criteria to make your proposal easier to comprehend for your readers. It can be tedious to read twelve to fifteen pages of design information presented in pure text, so breaking it up into three to four sections with subheadings—with each section addressing a different element of your plan—can make it easier to read and much easier for the reader to understand and remember all of the different elements of your plan.

NOTES

CHAPTER 5
MANAGEMENT PLAN

TIP 42:
USE A TABLE TO MAKE YOUR MANAGEMENT PLAN MORE COMPREHENSIBLE.

You will probably also want to use some text to describe your plan and supervisory responsibilities, but a table can address a lot of information in a small space. Consider separating the management plan for the first year of the project from those for the second and subsequent years because there are so many more details that must be addressed in the first year.

Sample of management plan table.

Activities	Timeline/ Milestones	Person(s) Responsible	Objectives

TIP 43:
MAKE SURE THE MANAGEMENT PLAN MATCHES THE DESIGN.

The management plan provides an opportunity to demonstrate, in summary form, how you are going to accomplish everything you said you would do in the design (or services) section. It is critical, however, that you are careful to include all the key activities from the project design in the management plan. You may want to write a preliminary management plan and then go through your design section, paragraph by paragraph, to make sure you have not left something out. Writers who lose points on the management plan almost always lose those points for one of two reasons: a) they left something out of the management plan that should have been there, or b) their plan lacked specificity, meaning they merely repeated the listing of activities without providing more detail. Try not to make either of these mistakes.

TIP 44:
INCLUDE A CONNECTION TO PROJECT OBJECTIVES.

Every single activity in your management plan should be connected to a project objective. This is important because the funding source wants to know that everything you will be doing with project money is, in some way, going to help you achieve your objectives. If you have an activity that is not linked to your objectives, you should ask yourself why you have included it.

TIP 45:
INCLUDE A TIMELINE FOR EACH ACTIVITY.

Your management plan should list when each activity will be accomplished. Being very specific is better than being general. Will a particular activity take place every year, every month, every week? When will the activity start? Will some activities begin during the first year of the program while others wait until the second or third year to be implemented? Let your readers know.

> *"We have time enough if we use it right."*
>
> *Johann W. Goethe*

TIP 46:
IDENTIFY THE PERSON(S) RESPONSIBLE FOR IMPLEMENTING EACH ACTIVITY.

Don't just list "principal" or "executive director" over and over again. Be realistic about who will really be implementing each activity and remember that it is acceptable to list more than one person or group if the responsibility will be shared, as long as the person with ultimate responsibility for the activity is listed. Keep in mind that you are not limited to people/positions funded by the grant. The entire staff should be considered. Also, use position titles, not names (unless the application materials specifically ask for names).

TIP 47:
BE DILIGENT IN THE DEVELOPMENT OF THE MANAGEMENT PLAN SO YOU CAN USE IT AS AN IMPLEMENTATION PLAN WHEN YOU ARE FUNDED.

The more careful you are in the development of your management plan, the better off you will be when you actually receive funding. If you think carefully through all of the implementation issues before you submit the proposal, you will save time later because you won't have to redesign your management plan completely. Of course, once you are funded, you will revisit the management plan to update it and make sure it is still relevant to your organization's current conditions and staff, but if you have been diligent in the original development of the plan, that review should not take very long.

I'll never forget walking into the office of a project director for a grant program I was evaluating. I had written the grant for that organization the year before and this project director was not yet hired at that time. When I walked into her office, I saw the management plan from the grant on her wall—enlarged to poster size. She was using it as a detailed blueprint for implementation. I was very glad that I had taken the time to create that management plan thoughtfully and thoroughly!

NOTES

CHAPTER 6
PERSONNEL

TIP 48:
DESCRIBE EACH POSITION THAT WILL SUPPORT THE PROJECT, REGARDLESS OF HOW IT IS FUNDED.

In the personnel section, you need to describe the positions that will be involved with the implementation of the project, even if they will not be funded through the grant. To include only those positions funded by the grant will leave the reader wondering how so few people will implement all those activities when, in reality, program implementation is a team activity. For example, the executive director or principal will not be funded through the project, but he or she will have a significant role to play in the management and implementation of the program. If a position is not going to be funded through the grant, be sure to include the funding source for the position and your best estimate of the percentage of that position's time that will be devoted to the implementation of this project.

TIP 49:
INCLUDE POSITION QUALIFICATIONS AND RESPONSIBILITIES.

Position qualifications are the required background and skills necessary for a person to effectively perform the job. Position responsibilities include the activities that the position will be required to implement in the project. Both of these are extremely important. It is a common error to list only qualifications or responsibilities rather than both.

TIP 50:
IF POSSIBLE, LIST THE NAMES OF REAL PEOPLE.

This does not mean that you should not list qualifications and responsibilities (see Tip 49), but including the name of a person already selected to fill a position or who is already on staff and meets the qualifications shows capacity. This demonstrates to the funding source that you are prepared once you receive funding because you already have some key staff members in place. Of course, it's fine if you don't have people identified for all your key positions, but surely you will have some identified even if it's only your executive director.

Some federal RFAs specifically say *not* to list the names of individuals. If this is the case, *follow those instructions.*

TIP 51:
CONSIDER USING A TABLE THAT SUMMARIZES ALL PROJECT POSITIONS.

The table will include the position, how it is funded, the percentage of time to be allocated to the project, and whether a person has been identified (name them) or is still "to be hired" (TBH). The use of such a table will make it easy for the reader to see your personnel plans. The table will not eliminate the need for narrative, but it will enable you to minimize the narrative and save some space.

Sample table to summarize positions.

Position	Funding	Percentage of Time Allocated to Project

TIP 52:
INCLUDE SITE SPECIALISTS AS KEY PERSONNEL.

You undoubtedly already have some specialists at your site who will either assist with program implementation or work with the project staff to coordinate new activities with existing services at your site. Including them in the proposal demonstrates your capacity to implement the grant as designed. Of course, you will have space limitations for your proposal narrative. You'll have to make decisions about what can be included based on the space you have available. The inclusion of existing site specialists in the personnel section may, or may not, be feasible.

NOTES

CHAPTER 7
EVALUATION

TIP 53:

REVIEW THE EVALUATION REQUIREMENTS OF THE FUNDING SOURCE BEFORE DEVELOPING THE EVALUATION PLAN.

Typically, an RFA will only minimally refer to the formal evaluation requirements of the funding source. You should visit the funder's Website or contact them by phone or email to ask for evaluation requirements. Your evaluation section will be much stronger if you refer specifically to formal evaluation requirements within your plan. This advance planning will also help you get a jump on those requirements once you have received funding.

Of course, if the RFA provides information about evaluation requirements, make sure you include those requirements in the evaluation plan you describe in your narrative.

TIP 54:
SELECT AND DESCRIBE AN EVALUATION DESIGN.

An evaluation design explains the theoretical and/or research frame-work you will be using for the evaluation. You may be using an experimental design, a quasi-experimental design, a modified time-series design, or any one of many other possible research designs. If you are unfamiliar with basic evaluation and research designs, consider purchasing (or borrowing) an evaluation textbook to help you with this. While you are not always required to name an evaluation design, identifying one that would work well for your project and describing evaluation activities that are consistent with that design, can make the difference between a credible evaluation plan and a weak one.

TIP 55:
INCLUDE A TABLE THAT LINKS EACH OBJECTIVE WITH THE DATA TO BE COLLECTED, TIMELINE, AND PERSON(S) RESPONSIBLE FOR DATA COLLECTION.

This table is part of your evaluation management plan. It will serve as both a tool for clarifying your evaluation plans for the funding source as well as for implementing your evaluation once you have received funding. Your objectives, which are the ultimate measure of the success of your project, are the centerpiece of the evaluation management plan. This evaluation plan illustrates how the data will be collected to demonstrate that objectives have been achieved.

Sample data collection plan table.

Objective	Measure(s)	Timeline	Person(s) Responsible

TIP 56:
CONSIDER IDENTIFYING SOME EVALUATION QUESTIONS TO GUIDE YOUR EVALUATION.

Evaluation questions are general questions that serve as reference points for your evaluation. Because they are worded in everyday language, they can also help your evaluation to be understood by your stakeholders. It will serve you well to pull together some stakeholders to develop a preliminary set of evaluation questions to include in your proposal. When you are funded, you will gather your evaluation team and staff to confirm your evaluation questions. To determine which questions you need, ask yourself, "If we are funded, what will we need to know to determine if we are successful and to continually improve the project?"

TIP 57:
BE SURE TO INCLUDE BOTH QUALITATIVE AND QUANTITATIVE SOURCES OF DATA.

In most cases, the RFA will direct you to address both qualitative and quantitative data, but even if it doesn't, you will want to do this because neither type of data tells the whole story. Quantitative data sources include those that are numerical or can be quantified. Examples of quantitative data include assessment results, survey summaries (numerical data, not open-ended summaries), and attendance data. Qualitative data are those that cannot be quantified. Examples of qualitative data include case studies, focus group interviews, and structured observations. Ideally, your evaluation design will include a blend of both types of data.

TIP 58:
DESCRIBE HOW THE DATA WILL BE ANALYZED.

You should describe technically how the data will be analyzed. Because you will be using both qualitative and quantitative data, you will need to describe the analytical methods you will use for each type of data. Consult an evaluation or research textbook or a professional external evaluator if you need assistance in this area.

Here are a few questions you should answer about quantitative data:

- How will you disaggregate the data? Why will you disaggregate the data in this manner?
- What statistical techniques will you use to analyze the data?
- Are there any specific statistical tests that you will use to determine the statistical significance of the growth demonstrated by the data?

For qualitative data, consider these questions:

- What specific information will you gather from the qualitative data that you cannot get from the quantitative data?
- What qualitative analytical techniques will you employ?

TIP 59:
INCLUDE THE EVALUATION OF IMPLEMENTATION DATA.

While outcome data are extremely important to your evaluation, it is also important to describe how you plan to evaluate the effectiveness of your project's implementation. You need to demonstrate that you have implemented your project as described. How will you know that this has been done? Will you monitor the number of program participants and the hours that services are provided? Will you ask questions about program implementation in your annual survey? What, specifically, will you ask, and which elements of implementation will you monitor?

TIP 60:

EXPLAIN HOW THE EVALUATION OF THIS PROJECT WILL BE LINKED WITH THE EVALUATIONS OF RELATED PROGRAMS.

In this age of accountability, there are multiple evaluations being conducted within every organization. Some of them are formal while others are informal. Ideally, you will want the evaluation of your new program to link with existing evaluations so you will not duplicate evaluation or data collection efforts. It is also important to use data provided by other program evaluations to improve your project's implementation as well as provide data from your evaluation to assist with the implementation of other organizational programs. Never lose sight of the fact that this project will be implemented within the context of a larger organization.

TIP 61:

IF YOU ARE GOING TO USE AN EXTERNAL EVALUATOR, DESCRIBE EXACTLY WHAT THAT PERSON WILL DO.

Part of this will be accomplished through the evaluation management plan table, but there should also be some narrative to explicitly describe the relationship between the external evaluator to the project and his or her role. How will the evaluator be selected? What experience should the evaluator have with this type of program? Exactly which evaluation tasks will the evaluator perform and how will he or she work with the program staff?

TIP 62:

IF YOU HAVE NOT INCLUDED THE QUALIFICATIONS OF THE EXTERNAL EVALUATOR IN THE PERSONNEL SECTION, DO IT IN THE EVALUATION SECTION.

If your evaluator will be playing a lead role in the evaluation, his or her qualifications are extremely important. Here are a few questions to guide you:

- What experience does the evaluator have with this type of program?
- What experience and formal training does he or she have (both in general and related to evaluation)?
- Has he or she evaluated other programs within your organization (demonstrating the ability to coordinate this evaluation with those of related programs)?

TIP 63:
DESCRIBE HOW THE ENTIRE ORGANIZATION WILL BE INCLUDED IN THE EVALUATION PROCESS AND HOW PEOPLE WILL PROVIDE FEEDBACK.

While many people think that evaluation is an isolated activity, the opposite is true. Think of the evaluation as a puzzle with many people in your organization each holding a piece. Each person represents a different perspective that is an integral part of the whole truth—how effective your program has been in achieving your goals and objectives. You need to describe specifically how you will include all stakeholders in the evaluation process. How will they have the opportunity to provide information? How will they learn of your preliminary evaluation results and have the opportunity to provide feedback?

TIP 64:
DESCRIBE HOW THE EVALUATION RESULTS WILL BE USED TO IMPROVE THE PROGRAM.

There are two types of evaluation: summative and formative. Summative evaluation refers to the use of evaluation data to determine the effectiveness of your program. It is a final determination of effectiveness. Formative evaluation refers to evaluation results that are used to improve the program as it is being implemented. Both types of evaluation are important and should be included in your evaluation plan. There are a variety of things you can do to use the results to improve your program, such as holding monthly or quarterly meetings to review evaluation data to decide how to use the information to modify your program.

NOTES

CHAPTER 8
BUDGET

TIP 65:

MAKE SURE THAT EVERY ACTIVITY IN THE PROJECT DESIGN IS INCLUDED SOMEHOW IN THE BUDGET.

This is very important. A good way to start is to go through the narrative, especially the design section, and make a list of everything you said you would do that is going to cost money, regardless of the source of that money. Don't forget things like child care, transportation, personnel salaries, fringe benefits, materials, and equipment. Then assign a dollar value to each item. Finally, determine which of the items will be included in the project budget and which will be provided through in-kind funds. Ask someone else to read the narrative and take a look at your budget to be sure you have not missed anything.

TIP 66:

IF POSSIBLE, INCLUDE AN IN-KIND BUDGET AND BUDGET NARRATIVE TO HELP THE READERS UNDERSTAND THE COMPLETE FINANCIAL PICTURE.

While some funding sources require that you include a formal in-kind budget and budget narrative, most do not. Even if it is not required, you should consider including one. Providing an in-kind budget demonstrates that you have put some thought into the coordination of related resources and that you have some capacity to sustain the program, at least in part, after the grant funding period. However, be aware that some programs require you to provide ongoing documentation of in-kind contributions as part of your evaluation or performance reporting process *after* you have received the grant. If this is the case, think carefully about how you discuss in-kind or matching funds in your budget and budget narrative. How will you know? You will know because you will have thoroughly read the RFA.

TIP 67:
USE YOUR BUDGET NARRATIVE TO FULLY EXPLAIN YOUR EXPENDITURES.

The budget narrative gives you an opportunity to explain how you arrived at the expenditures and amounts included in the budget. It is here where you will show your calculations and write explanations about why you need each item. Unless the budget narrative has a page limitation, use this space to expand on personnel job descriptions and the specific uses of equipment, materials, and supplies. Include the specific duties of any subcontractors. If there is a question that anyone might have while looking at your budget, it should be answered in your budget narrative.

Your budget narrative should also include your calculations. Don't just write that you need $2,000 for travel so the director can attend required grantee meetings. Explain the calculations. How much of that $2,000 is for airfare? How much for lodging? How much for food?

TIP 68:
MAKE THE BUDGET NARRATIVE EASIER TO READ BY ORGANIZING IT BY LINE ITEM.

If you are asked to provide budget codes, use those codes in the narrative also. You should organize the budget narrative by category and line item to make it as simple as possible for the readers to match the narrative with the budget. The categories you use in the budget narrative should match those you used on the budget form.

TIP 69:
CONNECT EACH EXPENDITURE TO A PROJECT OBJECTIVE.

If I have been sounding like a broken record by saying that every-thing should be connected to your project objectives, good! That means you are getting the point. Use the budget narrative to list the objective(s) supported by each expenditure. Remember the rule—if you cannot figure out which objective applies to a particular item, then you should ask yourself why you are spending money on that item. If an expenditure applies to all the objectives (like a project director, evaluation costs, etc.), just say so.

TIP 70:
USE EXISTING SALARY SCHEDULES TO HELP YOU DETERMINE PERSONNEL COSTS.

It is very difficult to know how much to allocate to personnel in a proposal budget. The best way to do it is to use a salary schedule for a similar position (or for the exact position, if you have one) and select the salary in the middle of the schedule. Someone with more experience or training will be slightly higher and someone with less experience and training will be slightly lower, but at least this method gives you a good starting point. If you know the job market in your area is tough, pick a salary toward the top of the schedule. The danger here is in selecting either a salary that is way too high (because the readers may wonder why you are spending so much on that position) or selecting a salary that is way too low (because you may never find someone for that salary and every dollar you go over budget for personnel is a dollar that comes out of your operating funds elsewhere in the budget).

TIP 71:
CONSIDER SALARY INCREASES FOR PROJECT PERSONNEL OVER THE LIFE OF THE PROJECT.

Consider building a cost-of-living increase for your project personnel into the budget. If you don't, you will have to deal with it later by taking the money from elsewhere in the budget. Also, addressing the cost-of-living increase demonstrates to the readers that you have thought ahead and that you have been realistic in your budget planning. Some organizations can commit to cover cost-of-living increases with other organizational funds. If this is possible for you, say so in both the proposal narrative and the budget narrative.

TIP 72:
CALCULATE FRINGE BENEFITS CORRECTLY.

Speak with your organization's finance department or bookkeeper and ask about fringe benefit costs. Describe these costs very carefully in the budget narrative and try not to underestimate them. Miscalculating fringe benefits can be a very costly mistake when you are implementing the grant.

TIP 73:
CALCULATE INDIRECT COSTS CORRECTLY.

Most funding sources will allow an organization to charge a certain percentage of the direct costs of the program as "indirect costs." These dollars go directly to the organization and are typically used to cover overhead and accounting expenses affiliated with managing the grant. Read the RFA carefully to see if indirect costs are allowed and, if they are, what percentage is allowed. Remember, the indirect costs should be a percentage of the direct costs, not a percentage of the total amount requested. (Direct costs + indirect costs = total amount requested.)

Some agencies now require that indirect cost rates be negotiated with the funding agency before they are allowed. Others require that non-governmental agencies (including nonprofit organizations) itemize their indirect costs. Read the instructions carefully.

TIP 74:
DON'T FORGET TO INCLUDE EVALUATION COSTS.

If you are going to hire an external evaluator, that contract should be listed in the budget. Even if you are not going to hire an evaluator, there will be costs associated with your evaluation that should be included, such as survey duplication and perhaps some extra duty time for project staff for data collection or data entry.

Some funding sources will give you an idea of the amount that is reasonable or expected to be spent on evaluation. Some even provide that amount in terms of a percentage of the overall grant (i.e., seven percent of the overall grant should be spent on evaluation). Regardless of how you determine the percentage of the total grant amount that should be devoted to evaluation, you should include that percentage and how you arrived at it in the budget narrative.

TIP 75:
CALCULATE THE COST PER PARTICIPANT.

This is a good technique to demonstrate the cost-effectiveness of your program. Divide the total dollars requested in a year by the number of expected participants. Don't forget to include all the participants (i.e., students, parents, teachers, etc.). This calculation should be explained in the adequacy of resources section of the narrative or in the budget narrative. If possible, compare the cost per participant for the newly proposed program with that of other programs at your site. If it is less, include that information in your proposal and pat yourself on the back for using funds efficiently.

TIP 76:
CHECK YOUR MATH. THEN CHECK IT AGAIN.

The most common errors made in budgets are simple math errors. Check your addition. Check your indirect cost calculations. Check your fringe benefits calculations. When you think it is right, have someone else check it for you and then check it again yourself.

I like to set up an Excel spreadsheet as I begin calculating the working budget. I program in all the necessary formulas before I enter a single number. This greatly decreases the chances that I will make a math error. Even after using a spreadsheet and letting the computer do all the calculations, I *still* have someone check all the numbers before the grant is submitted.

NOTES

CHAPTER 9
EDITING

TIP 77:

PROOFREAD YOUR PROPOSAL AT LEAST THREE TIMES BEFORE YOU SUBMIT IT.

You would be amazed at how easy it is to miss even the simplest of errors. Using the spell-check program on a computer does not guarantee there will be no errors. In fact, most errors these days are errors the spellchecker cannot catch, either because they are grammar issues (yes, even grammar-check is not foolproof) or they are words that are spelled correctly, just out of context. Proofreading is the least fun part of preparing your proposal, but it is probably the most important. Do not skimp in this area.

TIP 78:
HAVE MULTIPLE PEOPLE READ THE PROPOSAL.

The truth is that you are just too close to the material to catch all the errors. More importantly, you cannot be a good judge of whether your writing adequately communicates your intended message. Of course, it makes sense to *you*. The question is, will it make sense to the readers? The only way to tell is to let someone else read it and tell you what makes sense to him or her and what does not. Here's the important part—when they tell you that a description of something is not clear, don't argue with them. When your grant is being scored by the funding source, you will not have the opportunity to explain yourself to them. Just change it and ask if the new wording is easier to comprehend. While you may have to give up some of your favorite narrative in favor of wording that is simpler and more direct, it may help your efforts to secure funding. And after all, that is the only goal you should have. Period.

> *"A fool can no more see his own folly than he can see his ears."*
> *William M. Thackeray*

TIP 79:
GIVE THE PROPOSAL TO SOMEONE WHO KNOWS NOTHING ABOUT YOUR EXISTING PROGRAM AND ASK HIM OR HER TO REVIEW IT FOR YOU.

The readers will not know anything about your existing program, so you should have someone read your proposal who is unfamiliar with it as well. As scary as it is, you also need to accept that the readers may not even be experts in your field, so you need to make sure that your proposal demonstrates that you understand technical vocabulary without being so filled with jargon that the reader won't understand it. The only way to do this is to give it a test run with a layperson and modify it based on his or her comments.

This is one of those "check your ego at the door" tips. It is difficult to listen to and accept criticism, no matter how good you are or how experienced you are at accepting criticism. I still cringe when an editor insists that something I wrote needs to be changed, but I am grateful to hear it. Of course, in most cases, as the writer, I still have the final say. I can decide to take the advice or leave it. However, a smart writer takes the advice more than she leaves it.

TIP 80:
EDIT YOUR PROPOSAL USING THE SCORING RUBRIC OR CRITERIA AS A GUIDE.

Take the time to edit your proposal using the scoring criteria. Pretend you will be scoring the grant and read it from that perspective. If the funding source has not provided a sample score sheet, create your own to use. Did you address all of the criteria? Give your score sheet to your test readers and ask them to score it also. This will give you very valuable information that could make the difference between success and failure.

TIP 81:
FOLLOW THE 72-HOUR RULE WHENEVER POSSIBLE.

The 72-hour rule is this: When you think you are completely finished with a proposal (editing and all), put it away and come back to it seventy-two hours later for a final read. You will be amazed as you catch another error or two or find yourself rephrasing one or two ideas. Of course, this is not the time for a total rewrite, but you need the chance to look at it with a fresh eye. It takes about seventy-two hours for you to be removed enough from your own writing to have this fresh perspective. If you have pushed it right up to the deadline, try to give yourself at least twenty-four hours away from the document before your final review. This is not as good as seventy-two hours, but it is better than nothing.

> *"Many situations can be clarified by the passing of time..."*
> *Theodore I. Rubin*

NOTES

CHAPTER 10
FORMATTING

TIP 82:
FOLLOW ALL RFA FORMATTING GUIDELINES VERY CLOSELY.

Some RFAs are very specific and actually specify the font size and style to be used. Others simply mention the font size and margin specifications. Still others will give you no information about formatting. Be very careful to follow all formatting instructions, because to ignore them could mean the disqualification of your proposal.

Here are some formatting questions to look for in the RFA:

- *What font size is allowed?*
- *Is there a specific font required?*
- *Do the font size requirements apply to footnotes? Tables? Charts? Graphs?*
- *Are there line spacing requirements (single space, double space, etc.)?*
- *Is there a requirement about lines per vertical inch?*
- *Do the line spacing requirements apply to tables? Charts? Graphs?*
- *Are there any margin specifications? What are they?*
- *Are they any page numbering requirements?*
- *Is there any guidance for how bibliographic references should be handled?*
- *What is the page limitation for the narrative?*
- *Is there a page limitation for the budget narrative?*
- *Are any attachments allowed?*
- *Are there any page limitations for attachments?*

- *Are attachments bound by the other formatting requirements?*
- *Should the proposal be bound or stapled?*

TIP 83:
BE CREATIVE WITH HEADINGS, TABLES, AND GRAPHS.

Headings, tables, and graphs break up the text and can help you illustrate your points in a powerful way, but only if they are well done. The days of hand-drawn pie graphs are over. Make sure your graphics look good. The font and size of all main headings should match. The font used in tables should match that used in the narrative (even if it is not the same size) unless you have a good reason for making them not match. An acceptable reason for a font mismatch would be to make the text in your graph really stand out, but there are other ways to do this.

TIP 84:
USE AN EASY-TO-READ FONT.

It's very simple: the easier the proposal is for the readers to read, the happier they will be, and the happier they are, the higher your score. You may really like that Old English font, but it is so difficult to read that the readers will give up. Maybe you selected a very thin or narrow font so you could get more narrative in and still comply with the page limitation. Be very careful with this. Select a font that can be easily read. This decision will definitely pay off. Times New Roman and Arial (not Arial Narrow) are commonly used, easy-to-read fonts.

Serif Font	Sans-Serif Font
Times New Roman	Arial

More and more often these days, federal grant applications are specifying a font that must be used for proposals. Sometimes, they give two or three choices. Follow the instructions. (Have I said that enough yet?)

TIP 85:
BEFORE YOU MAIL THE PROPOSAL, DO A FINAL CHECK FOR FORMATTING.

Again, if you think I have been repeating this point about checking the proposal again and again and again, good! You are getting the point. Check to make sure that your final copy printed out correctly with the headings on all the right pages.

I do what I call a "final flip-through" before duplication and mailing. I print out the final draft of the narrative, and I carefully examine each page. This is not a final read through. That has already been done. This is a flip-through to ensure that all the tables break appropriately, that there are no headings starting on the last line of any page, that the narrative looks attractive, and that everything printed out as I saw it on the computer screen. I have often made minor modifications to a narrative as the result of a flip-through.

TIP 86:
MAKE SURE THE PROPOSAL ENDS ON THE LAST PAGE.

If you are given thirty pages to present your narrative, use thirty pages. Of course you know that you should not go over the page limit, but I suggest that you never go under the page limit either. Alter the font slightly, start each of your criteria responses on a new page, or add some graphics if you have extra room. While you will not be disqualified for ending your narrative three pages early, it may leave the reader wondering what you left out, and he or she may go back *looking* for something that might be missing. Everybody else will be using the entire allocation of pages for his or her narrative and you can bet that professional grant writers will be using every formatting trick in the book to get in as many words and graphics as they possibly can. If you want to compete (and you certainly can compete with that!), you need to at least make it look like you too needed every inch of space to describe your exemplary program.

The ideas I have just given you target using formatting techniques to lengthen your narrative, if necessary; however, the best approach would be to add detail to your narrative if you find that you have extra space. Look through your design section (or whatever section is worth the most points). Is there any detail you can add? If you don't have enough time to add any more narrative, use the formatting tips above to ensure you end on the last page.

NOTES

CHAPTER 11
ASSEMBLY AND MAILING

TIP 87:
USE THE CHECKLIST PROVIDED IN THE RFA.

As you assemble the final document, you need to be sure that you are
including everything in the order specified in the RFA. Don't count on this
being the same from year to year. Work through the checklist carefully,
checking off each individual item as you add it to the final document prior
to duplication. Every year the checklist saves me at least once.

TIP 88:
CHECK FOR SIGNATURES.

Check to make sure there is a signature on every page that is supposed to have a signature. Also check to be sure that the signatures are in the correct color of ink, if a particular color is required. Many funding sources ask for original signatures to be provided in blue ink because this helps distinguish originals from copies made in black and white. Some applicants will choose blue ink anyway because blue ink differentiates the signature from the rest of the black and white page, and the ink color is visible on electronic versions of the proposal. Of course, black ink makes a cleaner black and white copy. As always, follow the instructions and use your best judgment.

TIP 89:
COUNT THE PAGES.

After you have assembled the entire document and made your copies, count all of the pages in your original and all the copies. The only way to make sure that the copy machine actually picked up each and every page of the original is to count. Some of the readers will get your copies. Do you want to take a chance that a page or two will be missing?

TIP 90:
DOUBLE-CHECK THE MAILING INSTRUCTIONS.

Some grants have "mailing" deadlines and others have "receipt" deadlines. A mailing deadline means that you have to mail the grant by that
date to meet the deadline. The RFA will specify exactly what counts as
proof of mailing, but almost always a U.S. postmark is considered legal
proof of mailing. Consider sending your proposal as both registered and
certified mail. You will receive a return receipt when it is received (which
is nice because very few funding sources actually acknowledge they
received your proposal, and a little peace of mind can go a long way).
A receipt deadline means that the proposal must be received by the
deadline date (usually by a specific time of day) to meet the deadline.

Most federal RFAs now suggest that if you are submitting your proposal
in hard copy (as opposed to submitting it electronically using www.
grants.gov or another electronic system), you should use a private
commercial delivery service (such as Federal Express or United Parcel
Service). This recommendation is the result of disruptions to the U.S.
Postal Service that were experienced after 9/11. Some of those
disruptions continue today on a sporadic basis. When you see this
recommendation in an RFA, it is well worth the extra few dollars you
will have to spend for a private carrier to be sure your grant application
arrives on time.

TIP 91:
SELECT YOUR POSTAL CARRIER COMPANY CAREFULLY.

If you have pushed yourself right up to the deadline and you would like to use a private carrier (i.e., Federal Express or United Parcel Service), or if you are using a private carrier because that was recommended in the RFA, be sure to use one that you have used before and that you know is reliable. Before you choose a private carrier, however, read the RFA carefully. For some federal grants, the receipt deadline is modified to say that if you use a private carrier, you must mail it at least five days before the deadline.

TIP 92:
IF ALL ELSE FAILS AND YOU ARE OUT OF TIME, HAND DELIVER YOUR PROPOSAL.

Almost all funding sources will allow you to hand deliver an application. If you run out of time, you might be forced into this option. If you have to, just do it. While some people might think that buying a plane ticket or driving for three hours is just too expensive, giving up a million-dollar grant because you didn't want to spend $300 for a plane ticket sounds pretty expensive, too.

NOTES

CHAPTER 12
ETHICS

TIP 93:
TELL THE TRUTH.

This is simple, but it must be said. While some people choose to lie in grant proposals, including some "professionals," most people do not. You have to live with yourself, and you have to implement the grant once it is funded. Don't make the mistake of lying in the proposal. You will find that explaining yourself later to your stakeholders will be very difficult and that implementing a fabricated program can be more difficult than you ever imagined. Remember, *Oh, what a tangled web we weave...*

TIP 94:
DON'T "BORROW" SOMEONE ELSE'S WORK.

If someone else wrote a grant, you can learn from the style, the ideas, and the writing structure, but use your own words. There are a number of reasons for doing this. First, using someone else's words is plagiarism and it is wrong. Second, you might get caught. There are many funding agencies that are now choosing to eliminate grants from competitions that have a narrative that is identical to others in the same or previous competitions. Third, it is harder than you think to seamlessly integrate someone else's writing into your document. A good reader can tell there are two different writing styles, and if the reader is worrying about writing styles, he or she is not paying attention to the content of your narrative. Fourth, what if the person who originally wrote that grant was planning to "borrow" some of his or her own writing for another grant in this competition? The grant writing world is smaller than you think. Of course, if you *must* borrow someone else's writing, get permission and/or credit the author in the narrative.

"Let's not imitate others. Let's find ourselves and be ourselves."

Dale Carnegie

TIP 95:
USE THE PROPOSAL TO DESCRIBE WHAT YOU REALLY INTEND TO DO.

It is easy to be in the middle of describing your project design and then feel the urge to start elaborating a little. A little here, a little there, and suddenly you have committed to all sorts of things you don't really intend to do. Consider this tip a corollary of "Tell the truth." It is just as important. While the funding source is aware that some things will have changed in the period between when the proposal was written and when you receive funding, you will be expected to implement the program largely as written, unless you request special permission to do it differently.

TIP 96:

IF YOU USE A GRANT WRITER, ASK TO SEE AND REVIEW THE PROPOSAL BEFORE IT IS SUBMITTED AND HOLD HIM OR HER TO THE SAME ETHICAL STANDARDS THAT YOU ADHERE TO YOURSELF.

Don't trust anyone to submit the proposal before you have had a chance to review it. Make sure that it contains the vision you discussed with the writer and that there are no fabrications in it. It will be helpful to both you and the grant writer to set up a schedule for reviewing the grant and to include these dates in the writer's contract. When do you want to see a draft of the grant for first review? When do you want to see a revision for final review? Make it clear (ideally, in the contract) that you expect the grant writer to use all original narrative in your proposal. If you give permission for him or her to use some narrative from a previous grant your organization has submitted, specify that. A reputable grant writer will not be insulted at the inclusion of these contractual provisions. In fact, be wary of anyone who balks at being required to use only original text. That *is* what you are paying for, right?

TIP 97:
REMEMBER, THE GRANT PROPOSAL THAT YOU SUBMIT IS A REFLECTION OF YOUR ORGANIZATION'S CAPACITY.

While a funding source may not say it explicitly, it is understood that if you cannot put together a basic proposal, it is unlikely that you will be able to implement the program or comply with evaluation reporting requirements. The final grant proposal is a sample of the quality of your organization. It should be a source of pride.

NOTES

CHAPTER 13
FINDING GRANTS

TIP 98:
TRY THE FEDERAL REGISTER AND GRANTS.GOV

The Federal Register is the source for federal education grant announcements. While you can always look on other Websites, checking the Federal Register regularly is a must. Grants.gov is now the federal online center for grants for a variety of federal agencies (Department of Education, Heath and Human Services, and Department of the Interior, among others). If you are serious about finding federal grants that might meet your needs, you should check these sources at least once a week. Grants.gov will allow you to sign up to receive emails when any new grant competitions are announced.

TIP 99:
GOVERNMENTAL WEBSITES ARE OTHER POSSIBLE SOURCES.

If you are looking for education funding, you should check your state Department of Education Website regularly. The California Department of Education now has an entire section of their site devoted to funding opportunities. You can even sign up for email notification of new funding announcements. Other departments also provide grant information online. All you have to do is look. Many departments and agencies will mail you funding announcements if you call or write them and ask to be placed on their funding mailing list.

TIP 100:
LOOK IN THE FOUNDATION DIRECTORY.

The Foundation Directory is the place to look for private foundation funding. Most public libraries maintain updated copies in their reference sections; however, it is now available online for a modest fee. You can also purchase a CD or hard copy to keep at your office, but this is an expensive alternative and it probably would be worth it to you only if you plan on aggressively pursuing foundation funding. The Foundation Directory is a must-have for nonprofit organizations that depend on private sources of funding for their livelihood.

TIP 101:
SPEAK WITH OTHER ORGANIZATIONS THAT HAVE RECEIVED FUNDING FOR SIMILAR PROGRAMS, OR GO TO A PROFESSIONAL GRANT WRITER.

Talk to people at other similar organizations about their programs, how they fund them, and how they found their funding sources. You'll find they are happy to discuss the success they've had. Another option is to speak with a professional grant writer. Just as you go to an accountant for financial advice or to a doctor for medical advice, a professional grant writer can help you find funding. Grant writers are constantly searching for appropriate sources of funding on behalf of clients, and they often know of some excellent sources that would take you a long time to locate.

NOTES

ABOUT THE AUTHOR

Veronica Robbins is the Director/CEO of Creative Resources & Research, an educational consulting firm specializing in grant writing, program evaluation, and professional development training for schools, school districts, county agencies, and non-profit organizations. Ms. Robbins's many years of experience in the classroom, district and site administration, grant writing, and program evaluation are reflected in her phenomenal success rate in program funding, her insightful evaluations, and her powerful, thought-provoking workshops.

In the last decade, Ms. Robbins has written more than 200 grants with an overall funding rate of over 85%. In some funding categories, she boasts a funding rate of 100%. Her extensive experience includes state, federal, and private funding sources.

You can find more information about grant writing, grant management, and grant evaluation at Ms. Robbins's Website: www.grantgoddess.com.

CPSIA information can be obtained
at www.ICGtesting.com
Printed in the USA
FSHW010900060620
70967FS